"Having a wonderful time"

Picture postcards from 1894 to 1954

Gullane and Dirleton

Complied and edited by
Michael Cox and James Harrold

Published by the Gullane and Dirleton History Society 2002
ISBN 1 870479 08 4

The front cover postcard shows the Dirleton Castle Gardens
as depicted by R P Phillimore.
(See also page 42.)

Introduction

In 1995, the Gullane and Dirleton History Society published, jointly with the then East Lothian District Library Service, a book 'Wish you were here', containing reproductions of 47 Picture Postcards covering the villages of Aberlady, Gullane and Dirleton. These covered the heyday of Picture Postcards from 1894 to 1914.

Since then the Society has continued to collect postcards which provide more information on the social history of Gullane and Dirleton continuing up to the end of the 20th century. By last year a sufficiently large and diverse range of cards had been acquired to enable the Society to consider publishing a new book of picture postcards. The postcards in this book feature the two villages from the end of the 19th century through to the 1960s.

The growth of Gullane has been due to its seaside location with lovely sandy beaches and extensive links suitable for golf. Dirleton's beach, at Yellowcraig, is a mile from the village and its privately-owned golf course at Archerfield closed at the outbreak of the Second World War. As a result Dirleton has remained a quiet village drawing visitors to its Castle. Before the First World War Gullane

Golf Club had built three courses on the Hill and the courses at New Luffness and Muirfield were well established, the latter hosting 15 Open Golf Championships from 1892 through to 2002.

In 1901, the population of Gullane was 575. Significant development took place in the Edwardian period with new houses on the Hill designed by eminent architects such as Lorimer, Dunn and Mitchell. New local-authority and privately-built houses appeared after both the First and Second World Wars. By the Second World War Gullane's population was estimated to be 1750 and by the end of the century it was approaching 2400. Dirleton saw little growth during the 20th century. From 300 in 1901, the population was estimated to be 550 by 1939, but had fallen to below 500 by the 1990s.

Acknowledgements

Card selection, research and text by Michael Cox and James Harrold with photographic assessment by Geoffrey Quick.
Additional information provided by the East Lothian Local History Centre, the Myreton Motor Museum,
Sandy Barnes, Janie Carrie, Andrew Short, Maurice Timson and John Turbyne.

Picture Postcards

Imagine it is 1900, the afternoon is hot and all is still in the street of the village except for the muffled sounds of cattle from a nearby farm and the passing of an occasional horse and cart. A man, perspiring, dressed in tweed knee-trousers, jacket and a cap on his head, peddles along the street on a tricycle, encumbered with weird looking apparatus. He stops; dismounts and surveys his surroundings; unpacks his apparatus and assembles it; he is now ready to use his large plate-glass camera. He is taking photographs of the street, the village green, the church, the castle, the big houses, the shops, in fact anything that catches his expert eye. Another batch of picture postcards has been born!

In this book of picture postcards we see views of Gullane and Dirleton from the 1890s through to the 1960s. For local and social historians postcards often supplement the few surviving good photographs taken by amateur photographers before the Second World War. Although the photographs on picture postcards can provide historical information, their dating can prove difficult. The postal cancellation date stamp is of limited use, as postcards were often sold long after the photograph had been taken and the postcard published. Other checks have to be made to determine dates but these, at best, will only provide an estimate within a two to ten year period. However within these constraints the postcards in this book give some idea of what one would see when passing through the two villages from the end of the 19th century through to the middle of the 20th century.

The plain postcard was introduced in Austria on 1 October 1869 and in the United Kingdom one year later. In 1871 about 75 million of them passed through the Royal Mail. In the summer of 1894, when cards were permitted to be sent at the cheap rate of $1/2$d, George Stewart & Co of Edinburgh conceived the idea of the picture postcard and in September published a set of views of Edinburgh. From 1897 messages could be written on the address side, which, from 1902, had a dividing line with full size photographs on the reverse. A social revolution was launched.

A craze for sending and collecting picture postcards swept the globe, continuing to the present day. No parlour or drawing room worthy of the name was without an album in which to keep the ever-growing collection. In the year

1909-10 no less than 866,000,00 (yes, eight hundred and sixty six million) postcards of all types passed through the Royal Mail system - over two million a day and with no postcodes to worry about!

Scotland was to the forefront of picture postcard publishing with George Stewart & Co, W & A K Johnston, William Ritchie & Son (the Reliable Series), M Wane & Co, all of Edinburgh; Cynicus of Tayport, Fife; and, perhaps most famous of all, Valentines of Dundee. One name, of great local interest is Reginald P Phillimore (1855-1941). He was born in Nottingham and spent a good deal of time in his early years with his grandparents in Bridgnorth, Shropshire. Phillimore moved to Rockstowes, North Berwick in the early 1900s. He set up Phillimore & Co, producing distinctive picture postcards from his own paintings. In addition he published books on the History and Romance of the Bass Rock and Tantallon Castle, as well as Etchings of Old Edinburgh. In 1913, he published a Guide to North Berwick, Gullane. Aberlady, East Linton & District, drawing extensively from an earlier similarly-entitled guide written by A Williamson, one of twelve guides on Scottish towns issued in the Cicercone Series in 1907. There was also a separate guide for Gullane extracted from the larger guide.

Another local publisher of postcards was Ingram Gordon & Co of Haddington. In the mid-1920s, the proprietor of a photographic business, A Gordon, joined forces with another photographer, A G Ingram, forming the company Ingram Gordon & Co. During the next few years they produced high quality picture postcards of East Lothian views. They parted company in the early 1930s when Ingram set up a photographic business in Edinburgh.

There were a number of business ladies of Gullane and Dirleton who sold postcards under their own imprint but using photographs usually produced by well-known companies. Jessie Dane & Co. sold books of postcards produced by W R Ritchie of Edinburgh (Reliable Series) at her shop in Rosebery Place, Gullane. About 1906 Mary Eeles took over the business, trading as a China Merchant. She sold X Y & Co's Albany Series postcards.

Margaret and Elizabeth Munro had established, c1892, the Lothian Warehouse Emporium in Brighton Terrace, Gullane, selling drapery, gifts and stationery. By 1900, they were selling Reliable Series postcards. The two sisters moved to Stanley Road about 1910. Margaret continued the drapery business, whilst Elizabeth opened a separate newsagent's and stationery shop. Miss Munro kept Valentine postcards and later commissioned A R Edwards & Son of Selkirk to photograph views of Gullane. She died in 1924 and the business was taken over by her sister Isabella Lamb, who ran it until 1950. She in turn was succeeded by her daughter Alice Lamb who still lives in the village, after retiring at her 65th birthday in 1970.

In Dirleton we find A(gnes) H Reid of the Fidra Café selling imprinted Valentine's postcards in the 1920s. The Café was beside the village garage, run by her brother, Andrew, in the vicinity of the present village shop and post office. We have examples of postcards published by hotels, The Castle Inn and The Open Arms in Dirleton and Greywalls in Gullane. The postcard featuring the Drawing Room at Waverley House is another example of a card produced for a 'captive clientèle'; this one for the wives of retired miners spending a holiday there.

As it is over 100 years since the introduction of the picture postcard, members and friends of the Society welcome the opportunity to publish a second book of picture postcards. We have included many examples highlighting the part played by Scottish companies in this social revolution, and by visitors to this part of East Lothian who recorded their likes and dislikes when staying in or passing through our two villages.

G K Chesterton, the English novelist (1874-1936), once remarked that the dropping of a postcard into a pillar-box was the last romantic thing to do in the modern world. He was no doubt thinking not only of the picture and message but also of the complicated machinery of collection, despatch and delivery entailed in the sending of one of life's most hackneyed phrases "Having a wonderful time".

Gullane

**Described by R P Phillimore
in his 'Guide to North Berwick, Gullane,
Aberlady, East Linton & District' in 1913** .

"Breezy, healthy Gullane, beautifully situated on the sandy shore of the Forth is every year becoming more and more popular as a golfing centre and health resort. From ancient times it was noted as an excellent training ground for horses and there used to be a fine racecourse, the Gullane races being noted all over the country. It is in quite recent time that Gullane had become noted for its golfing facilities. Within a radius of half an hours' walk are seven of the finest links in the world.

From Gullane Hill may be seen an expanse of landscape and seascape unsurpassed for its own peculiar beauty. On a clear day may be seen St Abb's Head, in the middle distance Dirleton and its richly wooded policies, the farms of the Fentons and Saltcoats. Southwards are the Lammermoors and the Garleton Hills and the green cone of North Berwick Law to the east. Westwards lies Aberlady Bay and in the dimmer distance Arthur's Seat and the Pentlands. A local writer has well said, 'the view from this point would amply reward a journey of a hundred miles. Where we stand we look directly across the broad waters of the Bay towards 'Edina, Scotia's darling seat' and can even at this distance dimly descry her 'palaces and towers'. The shores of Fife, and the Ochils, blazing in the western sky, the 'noble Forth', with its emerald islands chased in gold, lie stretched before us'.

The Forth was once a favourite spawning ground for herring and it was not by any means an uncommon sight to see as many as four or five hundred boats within gunshot of 'Jovey's Neuk'. The word Gullane appears to be of Celtic origin. Fullerton in his Gazetteer of Scotland gives the derivation from the Celtic 'go-lyn' a small lake which would seem correct as in former times there was a small lake at Gullane. South of the links is Saltcoats Castle, its name being said to be derived from the fact that salt works existed at one time near the mouth of the Peffer Burn. Little is left of the Castle except the entrance gateway. The Coat Of Arms of the Livingstone family now finds a place over the door of the adjoining cottage."

'Catering for Visitors', as seen by Rev. H O Wallace of Dirleton in the Third Statistical Account of East Lothian 1953

"Gullane is essentially a holiday resort. It possesses a very fine beach in addition to its three first class golf courses. A very marked feature in the last 10-15 years has been the decline in the number of families taking houses for the summer months. This is thought to be due to the lack of entertainment facilities for young people, e.g. dance halls and picture houses. It would appear that visitors now mostly come to hotels and rooms. Good hotel accommodation is available in the village and good catering facilities are at the disposal of the public.

The golf courses are the main attraction. They are owned by the Gullane Club. Unfortunately the charges are considered rather high. Tennis courts were set up in 1927. There are no indoor entertainments. In recent years there has been a very large increase in day visitors, thanks mainly to the fine bus service from Edinburgh. Sunday sees the greatest influx. The local inhabitants do not look upon this as desirable, as the behaviour of many irresponsible elements tends to denigration of the fine character of the village. But they realise that it is impossible to stop this unfortunate feature."

Described by F P Tindall, the East Lothian County Planning Officer in a 1965 Guidebook

"Gullane was actively developed as a golfing resort in the early twentieth century and has many fine houses on the Hill. There are five courses, good hotels and boarding houses. Several roads turn off the main street passing round the Goose Green to Gullane beach, with its magnificent stretch of sand backed by high dunes. These dunes were rather devastated during the war, but efforts are being made to stabilise them. It is the finest of the many public beaches of East Lothian with a large car park. It is a very suitable place for bus parties and family outings and is visited by thousands of people each year."

*M*ultiview postcards were popular between the two Wars. Most of the publishers used illustrations of animals and bland captions. This is a 1930s look at Gullane with the beach huts prominent. These virtually disappeared during the Second World War when the beach was used for practising D-Day landings in early 1944. The houses on the Hill were built before 1914, many designed by leading architects of the day - Lorimer, Dunn, Mitchell and Peddie.

Gullane in the 1920s. The photograph of the Marine Hotel at the east end of the village shows a typical inter-war years telegraph pole on the footpath. The War Memorial erected in 1920 was moved to a new nearby location in 1929. The Smiddy is in action, but there is no traffic on the Main Street - just a lonely pedestrian.

*T*his postcard features Gullane just after the Second World War. The beach shows the ravages of naval and military activity with the dunes devoid of plant life. A successful regeneration programme from the 1960s restored the dunes to their former glory. The flagpole at the 1st tee of Gullane No.1 golf course was replaced by a simple pole, whilst the Clubhouse, opened in 1929, can be seen behind a tree which is still there today.

MEMORIAL AND OLD CHURCH RUIN, GULLANE (14)

*A*t the beginning of the 20th century the ruined Church of St Andrew was covered in ivy. In 1929 West Links Road was realigned at the Golf Professional's Shop to join the main road at right angles, with the War Memorial moved to its present site. Later ivy reappeared on the walls of the ruined church. Remedial action to remove it commenced at the end of the century.

This and the next photograph were taken on the same day within a few minutes of each other. People are waiting for a bus on what seems to have been a pleasant summer day in the early 1950s. The little traffic would have had no parking problems! We read that Archie, Molly and Kathleen were on holiday in Edinburgh and had spent the day in Gullane.

LAMMERVIEW TERRACE, GULLANE.

*L*ammerview Terrace comprises the new buildings in the centre of the photograph. Bisset's Hotel was built by a former butler at Archerfield House, Dirleton, in the 1890s. A rear view is featured later. An early Morris Minor car is passing the petrol pumps and garage, owned by Charles Lugton. Maggie sent this postcard to Charles McGilp of Prestatyn and said that she had enjoyed her day in Gullane.

MAIN STREET & THE HILL, GULLANE.   A 5360.

*T*his photograph, looking west, was taken mid-morning from a flat above the Post Office, in Lammerview Terrace. There is little activity; only one bus, van, car and cyclist to be seen. A similar photograph today would show many of the houses on the Hill obscured by trees. Marty had sent this card to a girl friend living in Didcot, writing that he and his parents were returning home that day.

MAIN STREET, GULLANE.

*T*his late 1940s photograph was taken on a lovely summer's day, with tables and chairs awaiting customers at the Wishing Well Café, later the award-winning La Potinière Restaurant. Elizabeth Munro had run the newsagent's shop from c1910 to 1924. The business passed to her sister, Isabella Lamb, and then to her niece Alice Lamb from 1950 to 1970.

The Links & Tower, Gullane

*T*his postcard dating from c1910 shows two substantial houses The Links and Tower. The latter was a hotel in the 1930s. A small farmyard with a house and cottage is seen to the left. Hill House (see next) sits prominently on Gullane Hill. Aggie sent this card to Mrs R Ross in Leith. 'We are having a nice time. I saw Bob's sister in N.B. yesterday, were there for the day'.

Gullane Hill House.

*H*ill House was built in 1904. It is a prominent feature when seen from the Firth of Forth and has been noted on navigational maps. Maggie wrote to Miss Wilkinson of Morebattle, Kelso, asking her 'to send on application forms so that she could apply for a teaching post'.

Gullane

Goose Green

Pub. Miss Munro. Photo by A R Edwards & Son Selkirk (3073)

Posted 3 January 1944

Goose Green, Gullane.

*T*his photograph taken during the early 1920s must have been a slow seller! The 1911 Coronation Tree was still alive and gas lamps still lit the streets. Writing from Seabrae in Marine Road, Ethel 'had a grand view of the sea all day long'. She would have possibly seen naval and military activity as the beach was then being used for practising D-Day landings and was out-of-bounds to all civilians.

*I*n 1900 members of the Episcopal Church in Gullane first worshipped in a Mission Hall, now the Golf Museum, and later in a corrugated iron structure at the east end of the Main Street. This, the present church, was built without a tower, in 1926. To celebrate the Royal Silver Jubilee the tower was added and completed in 1936. This dates the postcard to just before the outbreak of the Second World War.

This post-Second World War photograph shows Waverley House after it had become a holiday home for the wives of retired miners. Whatton Lodge in Hill Road was the convalescent home for miners at the same time. During the War Waverley House became an officers' mess and later a convalescent hospital. In the 1970s it became a local authority retirement home, which closed in 1999 against the wishes of local people.

THE DRAWING ROOM, WAVERLEY HOUSE, GULLANE   D 135

*T*his shows a typical 1950s décor with Lloyd Loom chairs to the fore. On the card opposite, B Ferguson writing to Miss Rigg of Falkirk wrote 'Having a lovely holiday here. The weather has been perfect. I am feeling a lot better. Kind regards'. On this card, 'Ma' writing to Irene and Willie wrote 'I am having a lovely holiday here. The food is very good and everything is just grand'.

*T*his is the rear view of Bissett's Hotel. The front view was seen earlier. It is a pre-World War II photograph which features a putting green. Nancy writes to 'Dear Mama' (Mrs Moor of Hutton, Berwick-on-Tweed) 'Arrived here about 2.40. Had a good journey but some long waits. It was very foggy all the way but is clearing now. Take care of yourself. Love to both'.

BOWLING GREEN AND U.F. CHURCH, GULLANE.

*B*issett's Hotel is seen through the trees. The original Bowling Club Pavilion was replaced in 1925. The U.F. Church united with the Parish Church in 1937. The unknown writer staying in the Pleasance, Aberlady, expected Mrs Robinson of Lasswade to visit 'on Tuesday forenoon and get out (of the bus) at the Bowling Green and come straight up the path through the little wood'. One would give the same directions today!

GREY WALLS HOUSE (ROSE GARDEN) GULLANE

*A*n early 20th century tinted postcard, long before Greywalls became a Hotel after the Second World War. It must have been one of Isabella Lamb's, slow sellers! Jean wrote to Tommy and Bob in Edinburgh. 'Family all down here for two weeks. This is our last day. Dad's third week on the panel. Mum was in bed also, the twins have not been too good either. Lots of love'. A sorry tale!

GREYWALLS HOTEL, GULLANE   D 5341

G reywalls, alongside Muirfield golf course, was designed in 1901 by Edwin Lutyens, with the garden by Gertrude Jekyll, and added to by Robert Lorimer. During the Second World War it was a military hospital. Opening as a hotel in 1948, Greywalls has always had postcards available for guests. This 1950s card sent to Harold Ray's wife in Sheffield told her that 'We are having an excellent time at this very comfortable house'.

"ALDERSYDE" GULLANE (HOME OF ANNIE S. SWAN)

*A*nother 1930s Tuck postcard. Annie S Swan (1859-1943) a well known novelist wrote over 150 books. She moved to Gullane following the death of her husband James Burnett Smith in 1927. Her home was named after her first novel 'Aldersyde' published in 1883. During her life she pursued a somewhat unconventional life - writing, speaking and travelling. She is fondly remembered as a prolific writer for 'The People's Friend'.

*A*nother 1950s postcard showing the Marine Hotel open for business. Used by the army during World War II, it did not survive long as a hotel after the War. It became the Scottish Fire Service Training School in 1954. M Robertson may have stayed at the hotel when writing to Mr W Russell and Lily at Newmains, Lanarkshire - 'Having a quiet holiday, the weather has not been kind however the change should help us'.

'Off For The Annual' overprinted 'At Gullane' - it could just as easily have read 'At North Berwick' or any seaside venue. The 'artist' Fred Gothard (1882-1977) worked in a bank and was a part-time illustrator.

The picture is titled 'The Sunshine of Life'. The artist was H B Wimbush (fl 1880-1908). A charming evocation of a bygone age. Mrs Fraser of Murrayfield, Edinburgh was told that 'Mr Matheson and I are here for the day'.

Dirleton

Described by R P Phillimore in his 'Guide to North Berwick, Gullane, Aberlady, East Linton & District' in 1913

"About two miles from North Berwick is the village of Dirleton, noted for its rustic beauty and claiming to be the prettiest village in Scotland. There is a spacious green, around which are cottages of the inhabitants, with red-tiled roofs and pretty gardens. One side of the green is flanked by the walls of the old ivy covered Castle. Fine trees are all around and near the post office is the entrance to the beautiful grounds of Archerfield House and in a retired corner is the Church and Manse. The former dates from the 17th century, although as early as 1444 a collegiate church was founded at Dirleton by Sir Walter Halliburton (or Halyburton), the first earl of Dirleton.

The Castle in old times was one of the most important in Scotland and was probably built in the Norman period". Phillimore then describes some of the military episodes connected with the castle but also adds some 'domestic' types of story such as: "In the middle of the 17th Century, when legal proceedings for witchcraft were so prevalent, a somewhat revolting scene occurred within the walls of Dirleton Castle. A man named Watson and his wife who had for a long time been suspected of witchcraft, voluntarily offered themselves for trial by a man named John Kincaid being an expert in the art of witch finding. As so often happened in these incomprehensible trials, the man and his wife made a confession of their guilt after Kincaid had found a spot on each which he could pierce without producing any sensation or issue of blood. The fate of the confessing parties is not recorded.

During the troublesome times of King Charles I, Dirleton Castle was held by 'malignant' Moss troopers in the King's interest. In 1650 General Monk appeared with General Lambert joining him later. They forced the garrison to surrender leaving the Castle in the state which we see it today. In 1653, the estate was purchased by Sir John Nisbet, a senator in the College of Justice and author of 'Dirleton's Doubts', a work that, in his day, was considered a legal masterpiece. At the present day, the Barony of Dirleton is owned by his descendant, the Hon Mrs Nisbet Hamilton-Ogilvy of Biel".

'Catering for Visitors', as seen by Rev. H O Wallace of Dirleton in the Third Statistical Account of East Lothian 1953

"Dirleton sets itself out in no way to cater for visitors by special facilities. Folk who come to Dirleton appreciate its picturesqueness and are captivated by its charm. The village green provides a fine setting for the old-world village. The beach at Dirleton (Yellowcraig) is on a par with that at Gullane. Its disadvantage for most folk is that it is a mile from the village. The approach to it is quite easy with a good road for about $3/4$ mile and after that rather rough going, but that does not prevent many people from coming down to the beach in their cars.

The inhabitants are always happy to see visitors, especially those who stay in the village for a week or longer. They view with less happiness those parties who come down for the day, particularly on Sunday, and make the common Green a playground. The action of these parties has also encouraged the (local) young people to feel that they too are entitled to play football etc on the green on Sunday. The hotels are instrumental in bringing many folk to the village on Sunday. In 9 out of 10 instances they have but one object in their visit".

Described by F P Tindall, the East Lothian County Planning Officer in a 1965 Guidebook

"Dirleton has the reputation of being the most attractive village in Scotland. It is built on a rocky outcrop and centred about a village green. The castle is set in well-kept gardens, with a bowling green surrounded by yew trees and a fine beehive doocot. North of the green the vista of the Church and its Kirkyard group well with the old parish school and school house. The carpenter's shop and smithy still remain. Dirleton is a lovely place for a summer afternoon or evening's outing and excellent food can be obtained at its two hotels. At the east end of the village a track leads down to the beach at Yellowcraig, where there is a car park and attractive places for picnics".

These five pictures could be purchased as separate full size postcards. Millar and Lang of Glasgow and London had a very large output that continued into the 1940s. Mrs Hogan told Miss Elizabeth Russell of Bathgate that they were 'enjoying our holiday. The weather has changed - see you at the weekend'.

This shows the west front of the house around 1900. After the Second World War, during which it had been used for military accommodation, it became a 'farm barn' and was virtually ruined. The cryptic message 'One for you' was sent by Agnes to Mrs Lamb of Port Seton.

*T*his baronial type house, designed by the eminent architects Kinnear and Peddie, was built in 1899 for John Ernest Laidlay, an eminent golfer at that period. Mr McInnes, Cheuffeur (sic), Glendevon, By Dollar received this card from Alice who wrote 'This is our house rather nice. Love from Alice'. Was she a servant and did she become Mrs McInnes?

*I*n contrast Ibris is a single storey house in Manse Road built in the late 1920s for David E Wallace, an accountant. Did he specially commission this card to send to his friends? His daughter-in-law continues to live there. The two halfpenny George V stamps are overprinted "Trade follows the 'phone".

The School, Dirleton.

*T*he school, opened in 1912, still serves the village today. The photograph was taken from the garden of 'Fairview' in Chapel Hill and also shows part of West End Cottage. Nothing has changed; even the telegraph pole is still there but without the wires.

We know the photograph dates from c1930 as three of the children have been identified (Adam and Jim Nicholson and Mary Shaw). The card was sent to Mrs D Black, Rothesay, by her daughter, Jenny, staying with a group in the school. 'We are having lovely weather here. We had races yesterday and I won a prize in the wheel-barrow race. It was a sewing set. Been bathing every day. We are going a picnic tomorrow'.

Castle Hotel Dirleton. Jas. Stewart

*J*ames Stewart was the proprietor in the late 1920s and 1930s. This group includes Stewart, Mrs Campbell of Red Row, two servants and Mr Ian Grant in the plus-fours. Was the card given to residents such as Frances writing to Mrs Mayger of Burton-upon-Trent? 'We are staying here until next Wed. Then we go to Edinburgh until Sat or Sun'.

ROUNDEL AND HOTEL, DIRLETON.   A.8752.

This photograph, taken just after the Second World War, shows the addition of a garage to the Castle Hotel in the photograph opposite. The scene has changed little, but the pavements, footpath and the green are better tended. Interestingly the card was sent by 'Dad & Jim' to Jim's wife 'Chrissie' who was living at the 'Girdleness Lighthouse, Torry, Aberdeen'. Dad asked 'Did Norman get measles?'

Dirleton Castle, *North Berwick.*

A tinted view of Dirleton Castle before the First World War showing a large amount of ivy on the walls. Complete removal of the ivy together with structural repairs were carried out after the War. The sheep pens alongside the boundary wall were used by the farmer at the adjacent Castle Mains Farm.

CASTLE ROUNDEL AND DIRLETON GREEN

A quiet 1960s view of Dirleton Green looking east, with cars parked outside the Open Arms Hotel. The footpaths and green are well maintained. The upper part of the Roundel houses an exhibition about the Castle with gardening equipment kept in the lower part.

*T*his is the black and white version of the tinted Phillimore postcard on the front cover. It is an Edwardian representation of the Castle garden at the height of fashion in carpet-bedding. More recently an example has been recreated in the garden so that we may know what our forebears actually saw. For information about Reginald P Phillimore refer to page 4.

A post-Second World War photograph showing a 'conventional' summer view of the now world famous 'longest herbaceous border', per the Guinness Book of Records. J M Gosdon sent this card to Rev. Mr & Mrs Broadfoot of Edinburgh. 'Having a very restful holiday in this beautiful little place. Weather has been perfect so far. I hope you both will have a good holiday at North Berwick'

I'm to be remaining here, all being well, till end of June. Weather has latterly been pretty cold, but is fortunately still dry. I sit out a lot in this lovely garden.

A CORNER OF DIRLETON.

211,923

× Inglenew.

*J*essie writes at length to Miss Brown, Castle Terrace, Edinburgh, to tell her that she is clearly progressing with her convalescence and is taking longer walks each day. She had been reading 'Freedom' by Jan Smuts. The circular group of shrubs in the centre of the driveway to these bungalows should be compared with the same group on the next card.

*T*wo more views of Ingleneuk and Netherlea. This card shows the two bungalows shortly after they were built in the early 1920s. Picket fencing is to be seen elsewhere in the village. Nancy, writing to Mrs Logie Robertson, near Wigan had also stayed at Ingleneuk. 'We have arrived and settled down and had a picnic at the beach today. I even bathed for about five seconds - awfully cold - but fine and sunny'.

EAST END, DIRLETON.

201504 (JV)

*T*his photograph was taken on the same day as the previous one in the early 1920s. We see fewer trees today. 'Dear Nancy. Enjoyed last week here, but the weather has been awful this week. Will look forward to seeing you. Write a PC to say when you are coming'. From the card we learn that both Josie Gunn and Nancy Robertson lived in Edinburgh.

DOVECOT AND END OF VILLAGE, DIRLETON.

292/10

*T*he dovecot in the Castle grounds is almost obscured by trees which are still there today. In the centre is the old bakehouse, whilst the funereal-looking horsedrawn equippage may unintentionally be reflected in the correspondence extolling the glorious weather and adding 'It is so peaceful here one almost forgets the war'.

164 War Memorial, Dirleton

Ingram Gordon & Co.

*T*he Memorial is on the lower green near the church and old village school (now the church hall) where villagers gather at remembrancetide to honour those men of the village who made the supreme sacrifice. This card shows the Memorial in the 1920s with the names of 31 men killed in World War I. Four more names were added after the Second World War. On the base we read 'They died that we may live'.

This is a black and white version of colour picture postcard of the then village shop and post office that flourished in the 1960s and 1970s. After it reverted to a bungalow the village shop and post office was, and still is, found on the opposite side of the road, 50 yards nearer North Berwick.

*T*his composite card of five photographs shows the hotel as it was known to visitors in the 1960s. The range of cars in front of the hotel mirrors the type of clientèle which the owner wished to attract - see next card. Hotels often published their own postcards for use by visitors - a cheap form of advertising.

A nother early 1960s postcard with not quite such grand cars as in the previous card. Margaret and Don wrote to Mabel Linton in Edinburgh 'Having a grand lazy holiday. This is a well organised Caravan Site (at nearby Yellowcraig) with all mod cons even 2 Showers. The weather has been wonderful 4 whole days without rain, what bliss after our terrible trip down on the Solway'.

Dirleton from North Berwick Road.   4.

A post-Second World War summer scene in the middle of the day, looking west towards the green, showing a sleepy village! A little girl going towards the school, one man on a bike, one lady, one car and a parked motor cycle. It is still a familiar scene.

DIRLETON CASTLE AND VILLAGE FROM EAST.   211,925 ⓘ

*T*he Castle is hard to find in this late 1920s photograph. Room for expansion? No road markings - the middle of the road seemed safe enough for the solitary early Austin car. The breeze would strum along the wires of the telephone poles.

North Berwick
THE LAMB.

A coloured card published in 1906 by Raphael Tuck and painted by Mrs Caroline R Stolterphot. It was from the set of four cards which the artist had published depicting offshore scenes in the parish of Dirleton, including the islands of Fidra and Craigleith.